JAMES RHODES was born in London in 1975. A keen piano player, at eighteen he was offered a scholarship at the Guildhall School of Music and Drama, but went to Edinburgh University instead. James stopped playing the piano entirely and dropped out after a year. He ended up working in the City of London for five years. After a devastating mental breakdown that led him to be institutionalized, he took the piano up again. He is now a professional and applauded concert pianist, writer, and TV and radio presenter. His memoir, *Instrumental*, was published to great critical acclaim and became an international bestseller. Visit him at jamesrhodes.tv.

Also by James Rhodes

James Rhodes' Playlist

Fire on All Sides

Instrumental

Others in The Experiment's *A Little Book On* series

How to Land a Plane
by Mark Vanhoenacker

HOW TO
PLAY
THE
PIANO

JAMES RHODES

THE EXPERIMENT

NEW YORK

Originally published in the UK by Quercus in 2016.
First published in North America in revised form by The Experiment, LLC, in 2019.

The Experiment, LLC, 220 East 23rd Street, Suite 600, New York, NY 10010-4658
theexperimentpublishing.com

THE EXPERIMENT and its colophon are registered trademarks of The Experiment,
LLC. Many of the designations used by manufacturers and sellers to distinguish their
products are claimed as trademarks. Where those designations appear in this book and
The Experiment was aware of a trademark claim, the designations have been capitalized.

The Experiment's books are available at special discounts when purchased in bulk for
premiums and sales promotions as well as for fund-raising or educational use. For
details, contact us at info@theexperimentpublishing.com.

Library of Congress Cataloging-in-Publication Data

Names: Rhodes, James, 1975- author.
Title: How to play the piano / James Rhodes.
Description: New York, NY : The Experiment, 2019.
Identifiers: LCCN 2018056926 (print) | LCCN 2018057188 (ebook) | ISBN
    9781615195497 (ebook) | ISBN 9781615195480 (cloth)
Subjects: LCSH: Piano--Instruction and study. | Bach, Johann Sebastian,
    1685-1750. Wohltemperierte Klavier, 1. T. Nr. 1.
Classification: LCC MT247.B18 (ebook) | LCC MT247.B18 R56 2019 (print) | DDC
    786.2/193--dc23
LC record available at https://lccn.loc.gov/2018056926

ISBN 978-1-61519-548-0
Ebook ISBN 978-1-61519-549-7

Cover and text design by Beth Bugler
Author photograph by Jan Martí Cervera | Illustrations by Amber Anderson

Manufactured in China

First printing April 2019
10 9 8 7 6 5 4 3 2

Chapter 1

Why do this?

Learning a musical instrument can unlock the door to a new dimension that many of us have forgotten even exists. If listening to music is soothing for the soul, then playing music is achieving enlightenment. It's going from kicking a ball around in the park with a few pals to playing alongside Ronaldo.

I'm going to make you a promise: This book will give you all the tools necessary to have you playing a piano masterpiece by Johann Sebastian Bach within six weeks. All you need are two hands; one, or preferably two, eyes; this book; and access to a piano or an electric keyboard. If it's a keyboard, then make sure it has at least a four-octave range and a sustain pedal (most of them will have this). You can get one online for under $60. Or you can buy a $100,000 Steinway grand. I leave it to you, although if you do have that kind of cash to spare, congratulations. And perhaps you'll invite me around to play with your shiny new piano.

Cooler yet, you only need to find forty-five minutes' practicing time a day. Bearing in mind the average professional musician practices four to six hours a day, you're getting off pretty lightly. Plus you can have one day off a week. Sounds achievable, no?

In the spirit of the world we live in I have made this method as simple, as immediate, as instantly gratifying, and as easy as possible. It's Tinder for aspiring pianists. By the end of this process (or awakening if you want to get all spiritual), you will be able to sit down at a keyboard, electric, or otherwise, and play a piece of music by Bach. You will be able to do this even if you've never touched a piano before; even if you can't read music; even if you claim not to have a musical bone in your body (this one is such a common refrain and yet such rubbish—I'll explain why later). If you used to play an instrument as a child but gave it up, so much the better; you now get to play again without a teacher haranguing you about rhythm worksheets, or parents guilting you over practicing your scales ad infinitum.

I'll be honest. What this won't do is have you playing Rachmaninov concertos and Chopin sonatas. If you find you want to progress to the next level after this, then you'll need to find a teacher and start to study things in a bit more depth. Part of me is hoping this book will act as a kind of musical springboard for some and get a few more people taking up the piano.

To make things a bit easier, and to help explain some of the more complex parts, I've made some short videos that can be found at jamesrhodes.tv—feel free to use these in conjunction with the book as they'll help you progress faster. You will find a copy of the sheet music inserted in this book. If you lose it, or want another copy, you can also download it from my website.

The piece I've chosen, Bach's Prelude No. 1 in C major, is only thirty-five bars long. And, rather cleverly, each bar involves only eight notes, most of which are almost always repeated to make sixteen notes per bar. What that means is, allowing for two bars a day, you need only learn SIXTEEN NOTES per day. I'm giving you a week to come to grips with the basics of piano playing and to learn to read music; three weeks to learn your bar a day; and then two weeks to join up those bars into one continuous piece and turn it into a performance.

Of course, if you're feeling inspired, you could easily shorten this considerably by learning three or four bars a day. The important thing, and perhaps the surprising thing, is how much you are going to enjoy the process of practicing. Trust me on this one.

But you might well want to take it deliberately slowly. We live in a world of distractions. We are working longer hours than ever before, facing immense pressures, and undergoing unheard-of changes in everything from medicine to technology. The society in which we live is moving faster than ever before in myriad ways, and as a species, we are struggling to keep grounded, let alone keep up. It's part of the reason mindfulness has its own section in bookshops, therapy is becoming one of the biggest growth sectors, and doctors are handing over mood-stabilizing pills out the wazoo.

The thing is, the lovely consequence of pursuing a creative activity is that, by its very definition, it looks inside of us rather than outside—it is a kind of stillness meditation for the soul. When you're sitting there at your keyboard, you're not going to be tweeting or liking Facebook posts, nor are you going to be assaulted by adverts, eating fast food, staring at cat videos online, or watching America's Next Top Model. It'll be you, focused, immersed, losing time in a good way, tapping into that potential we all have to release our inner creativity. Which is exactly what meditation does for us. And you end up not only feeling more chill and zen, but also playing the piano beautifully. A win–win. You might even get that girl or guy to fall in love with you, or engage your teenage children in something new and glorious.

Finding three-quarters of an hour a day to do this will produce profound results, both as far as your piano playing is concerned, but also in regards to your mood. The latest research (from Susan Hallam, professor emeritus of education and music psychology at University College London) shows that learning an instrument improves discipline, self-confidence, focus, problem-solving, language, literacy, math, and personal well-being. It increases the capacity of your memory, improves time management and organizational skills, enhances coordination, decreases stress, enhances your respiratory system, and promotes happiness in your life and that of those around you. Playing music can be an efficient way to stimulate the brain, establishing and strengthening new and existing connections, cutting across a broad swathe of its regions and cognitive functions, causing ripple effects through the decades (need I go on?). This is even the case "when measures of intelligence are taken into account." So you can be a complete dunce (waves at the camera) and still benefit from the fact that learning to play the piano makes you a more rounded and fulfilled person.

It can also make you more sociable, contrary to what you might think at first. You can do it with your children, a friend, a partner. It can be an inclusive thing that pushes back in some small way against our increasing isolation and our slightly alarming habit of forgetting to connect with others. There was a period not so long ago when, in the USA, there were more pianos than there were bathtubs. And I'm pretty sure that was a happier albeit smellier, less pressured environment. All of which makes it even more depressing that music education has all but fallen off the edge of a cliff in the last decade. The truth is that this book should not need to exist—every child in the country could and should be learning pieces of music like this as an integral part of their education. But governments have eroded music education and now we are beyond crisis point, and so it's something we're going to have to look to ourselves to achieve.

Time, of course, is the great excuse of our age. Forty-five minutes a day is, it will be claimed by many, simply impossible. False! I've gone to the bathroom for longer than forty-five minutes! Let's break things down a little: You get eight hours to sleep (I'm feeling generous), ten hours to work, four hours to feed the kids, get dressed, shower, etc. We have two hours left. A precious, wonderful, spacious two hours, and what do we do? We watch the latest reality TV show, complain about things online, sit on the sofa stupefied, stare at our screens, discuss the butt of the latest Kardashian on Twitter, anything to avoid being alone with our thoughts.

Enough.

Downtime is vital, of course it is, but there is room for all of it, I promise. I quit my job in the City of London aged twenty-eight and decided, having not played the piano for a decade (and being, at best, mediocre as a teenager), to become a concert pianist. Which, admittedly, is a little extreme. But I am convinced there is a middle ground where work and family responsibilities can be met while still finding space for our own creative pursuits.

So let's get cracking.

Chapter 2

The Basics

Go slow on this chapter. It's only fair to warn you that this "go slow" business is going to be something of a constant refrain in this book. You'll likely want to punch me several times, but it will save you so much time in the long term, I promise. You'll often feel like you're back at school with its attendant frustrations and sense of stupidity (it wasn't just me, was it?), but once you've mastered these basic points you'll be in terrific shape.

Here we go.

The keyboard

The piano has eighty-eight keys—fifty-two white keys and thirty-six black keys. The white keys represent the musical notes A, B, C, D, E, F, and G. The black keys differ from the white keys in that they represent half-step intervals—known as sharps and flats—between various notes. A group of seven white keys and five black keys together make up the twelve notes we call an octave:

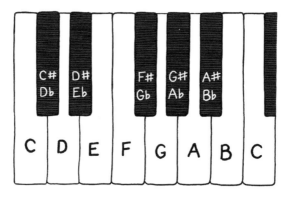

The good news, therefore, is that you only need to learn the names of twelve notes—each octave is set out exactly the same over the entire span of the piano, the ones at the lower end sounding deeper, the ones higher up sounding, well, higher.

These keys are the ABCs of the piano. The white ones are named from A to G, and the black ones are known as either x-sharp or x-flat, depending on if it is a half-step higher (sharp) or lower (flat) than the corresponding note name.

When you first start learning the piano, everything starts with Middle C which is, predictably, the note right in the middle of the keyboard and the best place to orient yourself when you first sit at the piano.

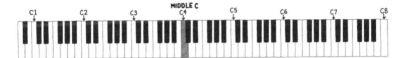

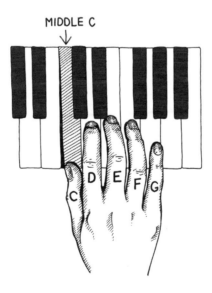

Spend some time now looking at the keyboard and exploring the notes, just to get a feel for what each note is called. Explore things by letting your fingers fall on random notes and see if you can name them. Use the eighty-eight-key image on page 8 to help, if you like.

Try not just the middle octave, but ones higher up and lower down, too, and see how they form the same patterns and groups throughout the entire span of the keyboard. It's no different (in fact it's actually easier) than learning where the letters are on a computer keyboard, which most of you can presumably do quite happily without thinking. Soon it'll be the same with the piano keys. The first step in learning the piano is being able to name all the keys on the keyboard. Please don't move on until you can drop your finger onto any random key and name it without too much hesitation.

Now you've got this, find an E (maybe the one just above middle C) and try playing it three times. Now play the same E three times again. Now play E, the G above it, and then the C and D below it and then the E again (see the following image if you need help with the notes).

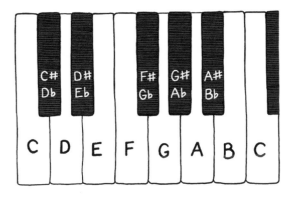

Now go and celebrate, because you've played the opening of "Jingle Bells," and because a day or two ago you wouldn't have known where to start had I asked you to do that.

What music looks like

Here comes the really important part and the one that will take the most time: learning to read music. And by that I mean that you are going to be able to translate black dots of ink on a page through your fingers and onto the piano keys, so you can bring to life something composed three hundred years ago that still makes the greatest minds of our world balk in disbelief.

Before you chuck this book away and think this is beyond you, bear in mind that children can learn to do this effortlessly and easily. So don't whine, just knuckle down and get it out of the way. It'll take an hour to get the basics, and a couple more hours of consolidating that info until it becomes natural. All you're going to be doing is learning how to read a new, simple language that only has twelve letters.

Here is how musical notation works:

The three most basic elements that make up music on the page are the notes, the staves, and the clefs. We know about the notes; let's look at the staves and clefs now.

Staves and clefs

With piano music, there are two staves on the printed page. Each of the two staves is made up of five lines and four spaces:

Each of the two staves is usually in a different clef.

Musical notes are set out on paper on two clefs—the treble and the bass clef. Generally speaking, the right hand plays what's on the treble clef in the stave that's on the top, and the left hand plays what's on the bass clef in the stave that's on the bottom.

right hand:
(treble clef)

left hand:
(bass clef)

The treble clef (right hand)

Now we're going to learn what each note looks like on the stave, and which note on the keyboard it corresponds to.

The notes on the lines can be remembered by using the mnemonic Every Good Boy Deserves Food (to be honest, all boys deserve food, but we can ignore the moral implications of this). The notes in the spaces spell out FACE:

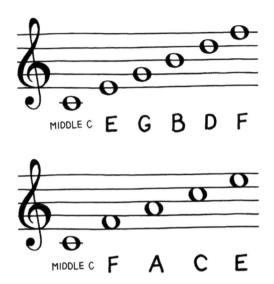

Now, you already know where these notes are on the piano keyboard because you learned that at the beginning of this chapter. The notes in the treble clef diagram above start with the E, which is two notes above middle C:

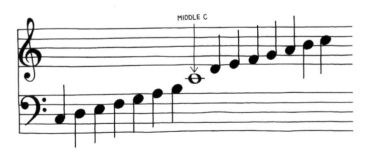

You'll notice that there is a note below the bottom line of the treble clef (it comes right above middle C and so, rather predictably, is a D). So make a connection now between the notes above and the keys on the keyboard—see if you can play the notes that are written in the previous image—first EGBDF and then FACE. Use the chart below to help:

RIGHT HAND

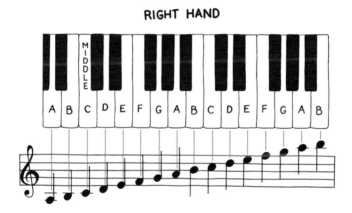

Please take as much time as you need to get a really firm grip of this. Think of it as the backbone of learning the piano—without it everything will crumble and fall apart. I know I sound like a particularly irritating teacher who was bullied as a kid and is finally able to take revenge by making others suffer, but it'll be so worth it in the end.

The bass clef (left hand)

The notes on the lines of the bass clef can be learned as Good Boys Deserve Food Always, while the ones in the spaces spell out All Cows Eat Grass (music teachers are obsessed with food). Remember that these notes all fall below middle C:

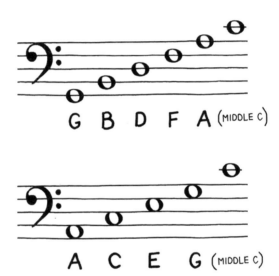

G B D F A (MIDDLE C)

A C E G (MIDDLE C)

You'll see there is a note above the top line of the bass clef in the bottom image on page 14 (the top line is an A so this note is a B). Again, spend some time figuring out which notes in the diagram above correspond to which keys on the keyboard, and try to make sense of how and why they fit together. Can you hear the melodic progression as you play the notes? The chart below will help:

LEFT HAND

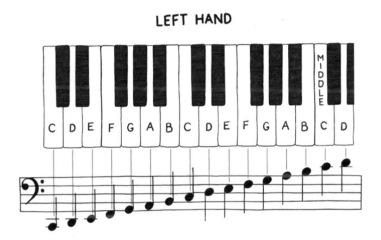

Here are both clefs together:

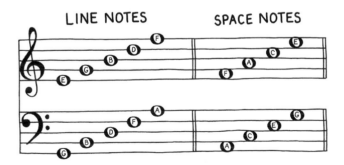

See if you can play all of these notes using the right hand for the treble clef and the left hand for the bass clef.

THIS IS IMPORTANT: Take half an hour now to connect the note on the page with the relevant note on the keyboard using the guide below. Use the left hand for notes below middle C and the right hand for ones above middle C:

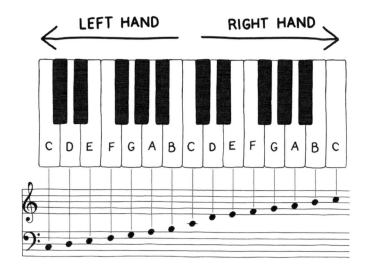

Sharp and flat notes

Remember how the black keys are known as either x-sharp or x-flat, depending on if they are a half-step higher or lower than the note name? In actual fact, we're not going to focus on the black keys too much, but you will need to know what sharps and flats mean and which keys they refer to, as some do crop up in this Bach Prelude.

These are the "sharp" black notes (#):

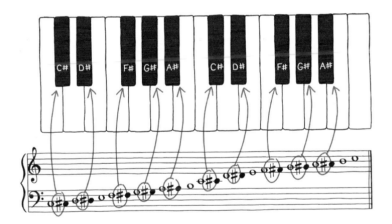

And these are the "flat" black notes (♭):

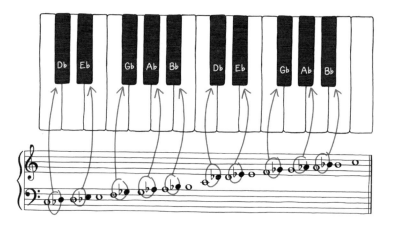

It is vital you can translate the notes on paper to the relevant keys on the piano.

PLEASE don't continue until you are relatively fluent in this. Once you've got this you will be able to progress much more quickly.

TAKE 5

Try this little exercise to see if you're ready to move on.

Look at this diagram and see if you can play all the notes in it using your right hand:

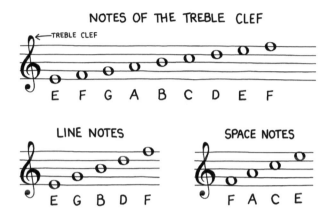

And again, with the left hand:

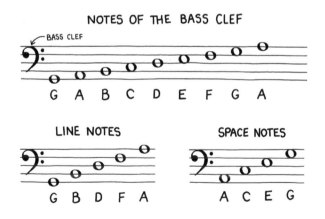

It's worth noting that there are seven notes that can be written in either bass or treble clef but which are actually the same note; there is some overlap here which can be confusing at times, but hopefully the diagrams below will make it simpler:

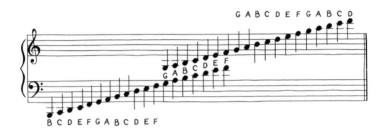

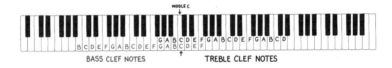

How long is it?

In addition to telling us which specific key on the keyboard to play, the notes that are placed on the stave also tell us how long to play them; i.e., how long you need to leave your fingers on them.

The main different kinds of notes and their corresponding rest value look like this:

NAMES FOR NOTES AND REST VALUES

SIGN	NAME/RELATIVE LENGTH	IN ¼ TIME	REST
O	WHOLE NOTE	4 BEATS	▬
♩	HALF NOTE	2 BEATS	▬
♩	QUARTER NOTE	1 BEAT	𝄽
♪	EIGHTH NOTE	½ BEAT	𝄾
♪	SIXTEENTH NOTE	¼ BEAT	𝄿

This can seem a little overwhelming, but rest assured that the piece you're going to learn has been chosen so that you don't need to worry about the difference between half notes, quarter notes, and sixteenth notes, etc. What you do need to worry about is ensuring you're able to read the basic notes. And bankers.

Also, you don't need to worry about things like "bars" (the length of the stave in between each vertical line), and time signatures (how many beats are in each bar, the beat being what you use when clapping or tapping your foot along to a song). As it happens, the piece you'll be learning has the standard four beats in the bar, which is all you need to know. I told you I'd make it easy for you.

TAKE 5

To recap—you can read music! Congratulations. This is amazing, it means that you know which note on the page corresponds to which key on the piano. If you don't, then please go back and practice until you do.

And here's a bonus point: What's lovely is that for the piece you'll be learning, you don't need to worry about playing both hands together at the same time. You'll be playing the left hand then right hand, and repeating the same patterns for the duration of the piece.

Fingering

So let's, without smirking, look at fingering.

The single most important thing in learning a piece of music is finding the correct finger to use for each note. You will be amazed at just how much time it saves me from spending countless hours exploring different fingerings when I'm learning a new piece, rather than just playing the notes however they seem to fit under my hands. Doing this not only makes it easier to play the piece, but it makes the notes sound much, much better, and it allows the melody to stand out more clearly. It also stops the hands getting tired. In much the same way as texting using one thumb will take ten times longer than using both hands, learning the correct fingering will make this Prelude both easy to learn and sound amazing.

The fingers of each hand are referred to by a number, with the thumb being 1 and little finger being 5.

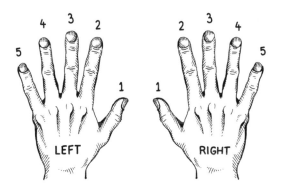

At its most basic, let's start with this:

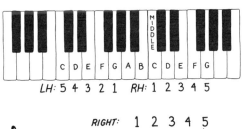

Let's try another one. Start by placing the fingers in the following position:

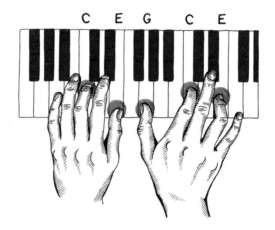

Left hand: C3 E1 (where 3 is the third finger, 1 is the thumb, etc.)
Right hand: G1 C2 E4

This is what it looks like on the page:

Now, play the notes one after the other very slowly. And again. Play it a few times until you can feel it being played nicely and evenly and at a decent speed.

Now play it again, but this time repeat the right hand notes so you're playing those three notes twice over.

You've just played the opening bar of the Bach Prelude No. 1 in C major.

TAKE 5

If you now know which note equates to which key, and can name all the keys on the piano and the score effortlessly and easily, see this:

and do this:

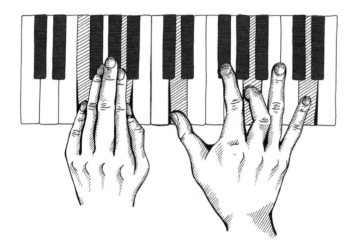

Then I am immensely proud of you.

What this means is you are now equipped to learn your first piece of music. If this prelude is the most beautiful girl or guy in the bar, you've now broken the ice, danced like an idiot, and yet still somehow managed to get their number. Now, finally, we get to the fun part.

Chapter 3

The Prelude

The piece you'll be playing is the first of forty-eight preludes that J. S. Bach wrote. He composed two books of twenty-four preludes and fugues, one in every key, and together they form what is one of Bach's most famous and enduring works, *The Well-Tempered Clavier*. He wrote the first book in 1722, and composed it "for the profit and use of musical youth desirous of learning . . ." So for you, basically.

It is a glorious piece, deceptively simple and offensively beautiful. People who think of Bach regularly (all sixteen of us) frequently make the mistake of assuming he was dry, unromantic, academic, and cold. False. Despite the fact that he fathered over twenty children, went dueling, got into fights and regularly got plastered on mead on a Saturday night, he also underwent significant emotional trauma. He lost most of his siblings, was orphaned by the age of ten, suffered serious abuse at school, and over half of his children died in infancy or childbirth. And his first wife, the love of his life, died quickly and unexpectedly while J. S. was off at a spa with his boss (in those days musicians were dragged along everywhere to provide entertainment). If anyone were more deserving of a spot on a daytime tabloid talk show it is Bach.

And yet, such was his work ethic and mindset, he ploughed on, unimaginably prolific, creating over three thousand works, teaching the organ and harpsichord, conducting choirs, teaching composition, writing music for the court and the church and for himself, taking church services, and generally putting us all to shame in the work arena. And this piece, this magnificent, gentle, romantic thirty-five-bar work of genius, is one of his many, many masterpieces. It's something most piano students attempt at some point during their studies, and for good reason—it can silence a room within a single bar.

So get your sheet music out, prop it up on the piano and read on.

We're going to go bar by bar here in groups of two. After every few bars we're going to stop and join everything together. In your score, the number at the beginning of each line refers to the number of that particular bar.

The really important thing here is to go slowly (sorry not sorry). I mean really slowly. So slowly you want to hit your head against the wall in frustration. Because if you can play this piece correctly ultra-slowly, you will be able to speed it up to a performance-level tempo effortlessly and easily. If you start too fast, you're not going to make it.

That way it all falls comfortably together.

A gentle reminder: Pay particular attention to the fingering before we start.

You're going to be spending more time on the first few bars while you come to grips with the process of figuring out the notes from the score and getting your fingers to hit the appropriate keys. Do not be discouraged—once you've got the hang of it you'll find it much easier going as we progress. We're going to ignore the pedal completely for the time being and the same goes for interpretation (how the piece is played, suffusing it with emotion, how loudly, and at what speed it's played, etc.). All of this will be covered once the notes have been learned.

I suggest you spend a whole forty-five-minute session on Bar 1, and another one on Bar 2. Then move on as quickly as you like. You can do four bars at a time if you prefer.

And make sure you look at the following treble and bass clef charts to remind yourself of which note is which, should you get lost.

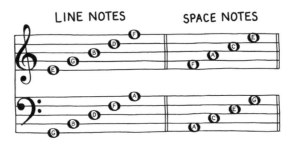

Bars 1–2

Have a look at the first bar. So, once again, your hand position for the start of this piece will be this:

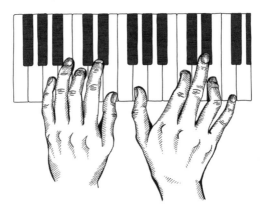

Notice how the left hand has the third finger on the first note
(C) and the right-hand thumb is on its first note (the G above it).

Let's practice the left-hand bit first.

The C is played with your third finger (hence the 3 under-
neath it) and the E with your thumb (1) and they are both then
kept held down (which is what the curved line, called a slur,
above the E means) until they are repeated. This is the same
throughout the piece—the left hand keeps its notes held down,
unlike the right hand, which keeps moving.

Play them both now, one after the other in the following way:

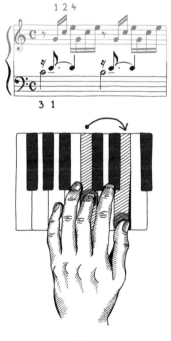

First two notes, wait for the right hand to play its six notes, and repeat.

Get used to that feeling. Easy, isn't it? This is how the left hand will be for the entire piece, a straightforward, easy two notes which vary almost imperceptibly at the beginning, and which are then repeated.

Now for the right hand where we're going to have a simple six notes (three notes repeated). And they said piano playing was hard.

Thumb on the G, second finger on the C above it and fourth finger on the E—then repeat. Try those six notes one after the other.

Now let's put left and right hands together. This is a big moment, so take your time with it. Get your hands in the right position, third finger and thumb from the left hand ready above its two notes, and thumb, second, and fourth fingers from the right hand ready above its three notes.

Now, very slowly, try playing the two left-hand notes followed by the six right-hand ones. Repeat the whole lot, remembering to keep the left-hand notes held down once you've played them.

Try that again now, still very slowly, and get used to the rhythm and the feeling of it. Although the notes will change throughout, the actual patterns of notes will be the same as these two bars throughout the whole Prelude.

What we really want is to have all the notes played smoothly and evenly without sounding hesitant or out of rhythm. This is SO important. Imagine reading a Shakespeare soliloquy where certain words are stressed unevenly: "To be or not to be"—the whole thing would sound ridiculous. Same principle here: The first note of the left hand is the jumping-off point and can be nice and firm, but the rest need to flow gently.

The best way to achieve this is practice. Slow, methodical practice. It'll be boring on occasion, but once you've got used to playing the first bar properly, it'll set the precedent for the rest of the piece. If you start to get frustrated, just think how good it is for your brain and well-being to be putting in that time and effort.

Now you've got Bar 1 down, from here on in it's just a case of learning the notes. You actually already know how to play them; you just need to make sure they're the right ones with the right fingering.

For Bar 2, the left hand changes slightly (although notice that the fingering stays the same). The second note is a D, not an E, and the right hand has shifted up a step so you're playing A, D, and F (with the thumb, third, and fifth fingers).

Again, practice this slowly, making sure you're using the right fingers, are playing the right notes, and at a speed that isn't hesitant or stilted but flowing, even if it sounds ludicrously protracted to you.

Bars 3–4

Same deal here: make sure you've got the notes and fingers correct and get to work. Bar 4 is the same as Bar 1, so you get off easy here.

TAKE 5

Now, let's pause and play through the first four bars. Take a breath, make sure your hands are in the right starting position and scan the first four bars before playing, looking out for any bits you find tricky. Then, slowly, start at the beginning and stop at the end of Bar 4. Repeat this a few times.

Bars 5–6

You'll notice quite a high note here in the right hand—working up from the top line of the treble clef (which is an F), you'll see that this high note is one line higher up, making it an A. There's a slightly bigger span here in the right hand in Bar 5, where the hand stretches from one A to the A an octave above it, so make sure you get used to that feeling. Bar 6 has our first black note—the F-sharp.

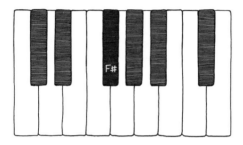

No biggie, just make sure you're using the right fingers.

Bars 7–8

Notice Bar 7 is the same as Bar 5, but everything has moved down a step. The patterns and span are identical, as is the fingering. The left-hand notes are the same as Bar 3, but note that the fingering is slightly different. Also, be aware that while the first left-hand note in Bar 8 is the same as Bar 7, the finger has changed from 3 to 2.

TAKE 5

To make sure these four bars you've just learned are consolidated, start at the beginning of Bar 5 and play through to the end of Bar 8 nice and steadily.

And now, just for fun, let's start from the beginning and play the first eight bars. Take your time, and if you have to stop (you will), do not worry. Just work through again from the beginning once you've figured out what was going awry (it'll be fingering or hesitating over the notes, I imagine). Spend a session just on these first eight bars, enjoying the feeling in your hands and the sound you're making.

Hey, you are nearly a quarter of the way through! Take a moment to congratulate yourself.

Bars 9–10

Bar 9 has the same right hand as Bar 8, but see how the left hand changes fingers and the notes vary from B and C, to A and C. Bar 10 has another black note (that same F-sharp again) and the left hand has moved down a bit further to D. That's why we're using the fifth finger of the left hand. Notice also that the mood changes a bit from Bar 9—there's a sense of moving forward now, and perhaps a little more urgency.

Bars 11–12

Bar 11 is simple, using the same fingering as the opening bar, but Bar 12 has a couple of black keys in it. Also, the left hand has a B-flat, played with the second finger, and the right hand has a C-sharp, played with the fourth finger. Just so you know, normally, when a note is marked as flat or sharp in a bar, then if that same note is repeated in the same bar, it stays as a sharp or flat unless indicated otherwise. But for ease of reference I've written in the repeated sharps or flats so that it's clear. Make sure you practice this so it doesn't make you hesitate.

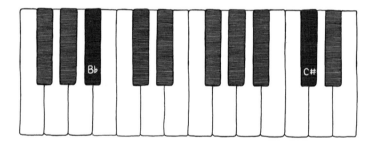

TAKE 5

Go back over Bars 9 to 12 and make sure you can play through these four bars comfortably.

Bars 13–14

Easy stuff here. Keep the fingering accurate and watch out for the A-flat black key in the left hand in Bar 14!

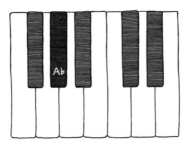

Bars 15–16

Again, nothing challenging here. In Bar 15 the right hand is playing just two notes again, C and G, and the left hand is playing E and G. In Bar 16 you'll notice the notes in the right hand have got a bit lower, starting with the A below middle C. This is the start of a really incredible moment that lasts a few bars; you'll see what I mean as you move ahead, but this is where just a little bit of tension begins to creep in for the first time in this piece.

Bars 17–18

Notice how the right hand of Bar 17 is identical to the preceding bar. The left hand drops one note and then falls a bit lower to the G at the beginning of Bar 18 (double-check your fingering here!), while the right hand in Bar 18 also drops to G, one of the lowest notes it'll play in the piece.

TAKE 5

Here's something challenging and brilliant for you. We are just over halfway through now, and I want you to play the entire first half from start to finish.

Take it slowly, as always, and see if you can get through the whole first eighteen bars. It may take some time and a few attempts, but if you can, then HUGE congratulations. Don't worry about what it sounds like—just focus on making sure the notes and fingering are correct. Think of it as musical foreplay—I promise you, once you've got the notes down, the performance will follow effortlessly.

Take a moment to notice how Bach has gradually taken you from the gentle, optimistic heights of the first bars to heavier sounds and the notes moving further down the keyboard. To use that awful word, beloved of TV execs everywhere, he's taking us on a journey; now we're settled in, and it's going to start to get a bit funkier, in a really good way.

Bars 19–20

Bar 19 is the same as the opening bar, just an octave lower. Easy. Watch out for the black note (B-flat) in Bar 20.

Bars 21–22

Bar 21 has the biggest stretch in the piece for the left hand—a whole octave between F and F. Unless you've got freakishly small hands, it won't be a problem to use the fingering marked on the score. Bar 22 is the same as Bar 21 for the right hand, except for the E-flat. Watch out for the left-hand notes, which begins with an F-sharp.

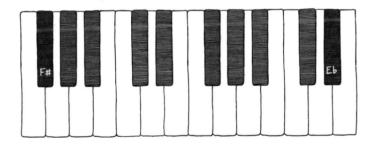

TAKE 5

Pause here and go through the last four bars, 19 to 22, and make sure they flow.

Bars 23–24

Again, check your fingering (have I made it clear how important this is yet?!), but nothing too tricky here, except for the A-flat at the beginning of Bar 23.

Bars 25–26

Simple, simple.

Bars 27–28

Bar 28 could trip you up a little, as the left hand has quite an awkward stretch from the G to the E-flat, so double-check you've got the right notes and right fingering, and practice the left-hand solo for a bit.

TAKE 5

Once you've got Bar 28 sorted, go back to Bar 23 and play through these six bars.

Bars 29–30

Bar 29 has our first (and only) weird symbol, ♮. Don't worry about this. It just means that the left-hand E is a white note (an E natural, it's called) and not an E-flat, as in the previous bar. Bach uses it to start to diffuse the tension of the previous bar, which is quite gnarly, harmonically speaking.

Bars 31–32

The left hand changes finger halfway through Bar 31 to make sure the move from the G to the C below it, in Bar 32, is easier. That C in Bar 32 is the lowest note in the piece and you know it's a C by counting down from the G in the previous bar. It's another big stretch. And do watch out for that B-flat in the right hand.

Almost there, only three more bars to go!

Bars 33–34

I'm not gonna lie; these guys are going to take some work. I know that visually, they look daunting, too. It is very doable though. The only reason it seems difficult at first glance is because the pattern has changed—up until now every bar has followed the same structure, but these two bars are slightly different and will involve changing the right hand's position and fingering in a new way compared to what has come before.

Let's break it down—and remember to go to my website for some explanatory videos.

Bar 33

The first half of this bar is pretty simple; it's just slightly changed its pattern from the previous bars. The left hand is identical to the previous bar.

The second half will be easy IF you make sure you use the fingering I've given you! Even though it's written in the bass clef, you can play it all with the right hand. The most important thing to work on is playing the second A with the fourth finger instead of the second finger. So practice it super slowly until both the fingering AND the change in note pattern feel natural to you.

Bar 34

Similarly, the left hand here is a simple C to B. The right hand will be easy if you practice it at a snail's pace, like you did in the bar before, and make sure you use the correct fingering.

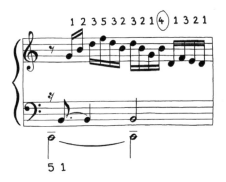

Bar 35

Here is the first time we are playing both hands together and more than one note at a time. In fact you're going to finish the whole piece now on a single C-major chord. This is Bach's way of coming back full circle to the opening of the piece and ending on a high. It's really not difficult; this is what it looks like:

You'll be playing the C, G, and E at the same time with the right hand as shown in the previous illustration, and the left hand will be playing both Cs at the same time, too.

The important thing to practice, once you're used to playing this chord all together, is the link between the very last note of the bar before, and the chord itself. It needs to be smooth and joined up, with no gap. You'll see that the last note of the previous bar is played with the right-hand thumb, and the chord's bottom right-hand note is played with the second finger. This is so you can join them up together easily.

So practice this:

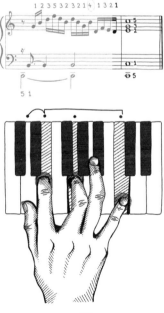

until you're blue in the face—you really want to end on a glorious, harmonic high!

Make sure all the notes sound at the same time, and that all of the notes are played at the same volume—we want to avoid, say, the left hand being really loud and overpowering the chord in the right hand. This is a lovely, clear, C-major end to the piece, and should be balanced nice and evenly.

Spend as long as it takes on these last two bars as they are really, really crucial. And when you've got them nailed, then play the last six bars (Bars 30–35) and make sure they're sorted.

TAKE 5

Now we can go through the second half of the piece (Bar 19 to the end) and stitch it all together like we did the first half. Don't hurry. Whenever you hit a wall, STOP, and figure out what the issue is. Solve the problem before moving on.

Finally, let's go for the whole thing from beginning to end.

The best way to do this is to play it slowly (how did you know I was going to say that?). Pay particular attention to the joins between each bar, as we want these to be as smooth as possible. Think of the whole piece as one long bar that flows effortlessly from beginning to end. It will inevitably sound a bit disjointed, playing it through without pedal. That's fine. Just make sure your fingering is correct and that the notes all flow without interruption or hesitation. As ever, if you reach a passage that you find difficult for any reason, then stop, go back, and go over it again and again until it flows.

If you can do this, then you are nearly there and have made immense progress. Take some time out now and celebrate—perhaps nonchalantly inform your significant other/friends/kids that you've almost finished learning a new piece of Bach, and allow yourself to feel slightly smug because, well, it's a remarkable accomplishment. Acknowledge what you have achieved by this stage; you've gone from not having played the piano in years (or ever) to learning how to read music and performing, albeit slowly, a piece of music that is performed around the world every day by concert pianists. Boom!

Chapter 4

The Performance

Why use pedals?

One of the things that will really help turn this into a performance is the pedal.

Most traditional pianos have two pedals: The right one sustains notes, and the left one dampens or quietens them. The majority of electric keyboards have a sustain pedal (although you may need to buy one). Try playing the first couple of bars, using the sustain pedal at the start of every bar. As you press the first note down, press the right pedal down at the same time and keep it held down. At the very start of the next bar, lift your foot up and put it back down quickly so that the join is nice and smooth.

The trap to avoid is blurring the notes by using the sustain pedal too much, or by not lifting it up and putting it back down in the right place. Spend some time coming to grips with the technique. If you release it and then reapply it in the right way (and you can do this in the blink of an eye) then there shouldn't be any noticeable joins between the notes.

Listen to the sound you're making (you could record yourself on your phone and listen back) and try to ensure it doesn't seem blurry.

If you want to use the soft pedal in places, feel free. It's a lovely, easy way to make the sound a bit quieter as and when you feel it necessary, and something you'll probably want to use a bit more once you've got your head around interpretation.

But before we move on to that subject, I want you to get the piece up to speed. The only way to do this is by starting slowly, and gradually increasing the tempo. Go at your own pace and spend a day or two building it up to a nice steady speed. Use the pedals and enjoy this process—have a look at my videos about this, as they will help you.

Interpretation

So, you can now play through the whole score, at a decent tempo, and without too much hesitation or faltering. The pedal should allow you to make sure it's smooth, but not indistinct. And now we get to go from playing the notes to giving a performance.

People often say there's no way to teach musicality; it's something you either have or don't have. I think that is true. But I also think that everyone is born with an inherent musicality. It is part of our makeup; if you are capable of feeling a certain way while listening to a song or piece of music, then you have an innate musicality. It's now time to express that.

Bach was very unspecific about how his pieces should be played. From Mozart and Beethoven onwards, there were countless directions regarding speed, volume, phrasing, etc., but Bach sometimes didn't even specify what instrument a piece should be played on, let alone what tempo should be adopted. Which is ace, because that allows us to play it exactly as we feel best expresses the composition without worrying about going against the composer's wishes.

The best way to access the interpretation you feel really works is simply to sit and play through the music in your head. Whistle it, sing it, play it over again and again in your mind, and see what makes you feel good (try and avoid doing this on the subway if possible—it's not a great look). It may be you like a nice, slow pace with lots of pedal, making it sound romantic, or you may prefer a livelier, faster pace with very little pedal. You might want to decide if you'd like the first note of the left hand to be the dominant one, as far as the melody is concerned, or perhaps you feel the last note of the right hand works best in that regard. Play around with it! Explore and experiment, and enjoy the sense of freedom it can give you. Think of it as a form of meditation, with no right or wrong way.

Do listen to recordings of this piece. There are dozens on YouTube and Spotify. Find some that you like, and ask yourself why it is that you prefer specific ones. Is it the tempo, the way a pianist might slow things down or ramp them up? The feeling that the pianist imbues it with? The volume it's played at (some performances of this piece are very softly played, while others are more brittle)? Or is it the cheesy autumnal landscapes and moody shots of waterfalls that seem to be used all the bloody time with music like this on YouTube? (In which case, seek help.) A few great recordings that I'd recommend are Glenn Gould, Friedrich Gulda, Hélène Grimaud, and Grigory Sokolov (all on YouTube). Listen to these and see the immense difference in speed, tone, feeling in all of them—there's so much room for individuality.

Look at Bars 5 and 6. Here there seems to be a dialogue between two different registers of the piano. Bar 5 should be perhaps a little louder, and then Bar 6 answers it more quietly. This is then repeated in Bars 7 and 8—the same thing, Bar 7 louder, Bar 8 responding more quietly.

Or take Bars 24 to 30. Try playing these bars starting quietly and getting louder and louder. You can hear the pressure ramping up in the music, and there is a natural, unspoken need to get louder as it does so—and then the volume, to my mind, needs to subside around Bars 30 to 31.

Have fun exploring the score, living with it for a while, breathing it in and submerging yourself in it, finding what works for you. That may sound too much, even a little ridiculous, but, as the late, great E. M. Forster said, this kind of music is "the deepest of the arts and deep beneath the arts." We can sink into it and use it as an escape, a place beyond thinking. And God knows we need more of that.

Figure out what you love in certain performances and see if that's the way you would like to play the piece. Try and emulate the performance in your practice, and maybe use it as a springboard to find your own interpretation.

TAKE 5

You may well find that you can remember the notes now and put the sheet music to one side. When we practice correctly it's amazing how much goes into the brain without us realizing. There is no need to learn it by heart, but if you want to and you need a bit of help, try the following (these are things that I do myself to memorize and prepare for concerts).

Start playing the piece from memory, at least half the performance speed. When you hit a bar that you've forgotten, stop. Check the score and make sure you can memorize that specific bar, then go back two or three bars before and play through to a couple of bars after the problem bar. Repeat until you've got it. If you can play a piece from memory at half speed, you'll have no problem at full speed. Think of yourself as an actor learning a monologue; if she can pause for a second between each word and get through it correctly, it's safe to say she knows it inside out.

Another great tip is to practice away from the piano. It is amazing just how much work can be done in this way. See your hands at the keyboard in your mind's eye and play through the piece without physically moving them as you do this. Try and see each note on the keyboard as you play it; any time you hit a blank, stop, go back to the score and study the problem until you've got the solution down.

Chapter 5

What happens now?

Let's finish by taking a moment to notice how far you have come.

You should now be able to play the piece through from beginning to end, maybe even from memory. You have an idea in your mind about what it should sound like and what you want it to sound like, and you can, using the pedal, your own innate musicality, and slow practice, translate that idea into reality. You can perform this piece in its entirety.

In the space of a few short weeks, through dedication, focus, and hard work, you have gone from barely playing a note to performing Bach on the piano. It's an astonishing, epic, magnificent achievement.

Think about what that means. Instead of showing your friends the 1,000 photos you took on your last holiday in Sicily, or spending hours spiralizing zucchinis and carrots for a dinner party, you can play them this piece!

A quick word about nerves. You may find, when playing the piano for other people, that it feels different from playing it for yourself; dry mouth, shaking hands, that annoying inner voice saying you're going to mess it up. This is entirely, irritatingly normal. This happens to me frequently on stage. The way around it is by accepting fully that you know this piece. You have spent weeks working on it—you have studied every single note—and you can, without a doubt, play it. So if, when it comes to performing it for someone or a small group of friends, you feel nervous, simply look at it as if you are going to do something effortless like watching a movie together or taking a walk. You wouldn't get nervous about those things, you'd enjoy them and look forward to them. Same applies here—there is no need for nerves—you can simply have fun doing something that is as easy to you as meeting a couple of friends for dinner somewhere. The more you look at it from this perspective, the easier it will be to perform. It's remarkable how we can train the mind not to unravel (sometimes).

Maybe you'll want to upload your performance to YouTube. Feel free to send it to me on Twitter, or simply bask in the fact that you've done something extraordinary. Perhaps you'll want to learn Beethoven next; for example, the first movement of the *Moonlight Sonata*, or Chopin's Prelude No. 4 in E minor. You might want to find a decent piano teacher and move forward with them, exploring the piano on a deeper level. Or maybe you've done what you set out to do, and that's good enough. Either way, I wish you well and am so happy you've taken such a brave and brilliant first step back into creativity. Perhaps one day I'll be lucky enough to see you perform.

Bach himself said, "It's easy to play any musical instrument: all you have to do is touch the right key at the right time and the instrument will play itself." And, while he was perhaps (OK, definitely) being a bit obtuse, you are now, through your own hard work, able to touch the right key at the right time. What a brilliant thing to have accomplished.